HOLDING SPACE

A companion Journal

By

Deidra Jackson

© 2025 Deidra Jackson. All rights reserved.

No portion of this book may be reproduced in any form without permission from the author.

Self-Published by Deidra Jackson

Printed in the United States of America.

First Edition

ISBN: 979-8-9937862-2-3

For Dad ---
 Who always said,
"Danielle, strangers are only friends I haven't met yet"

Welcome, friend.

Date: _____

Holding Space For: _____

Holding Space

_____
_____
_____
_____
_____
_____
_____
_____
_____
_____
_____
_____
_____
_____
_____
_____
_____
_____
_____
_____
_____
_____
_____
_____

"Caregiving wears differently than exhaustion. It's a quiet erosion of margins."

Date: _____

Holding Space For: _____

Date: _____

Holding Space For: _____

Date: _____

Holding Space For: _____

Date: _____

Holding Space For: _____

Date: _____

Holding Space For: _____

Date: _____

Holding Space For: _____

Date: _____

Holding Space For: _____

Date: _____

Holding Space For: _____

_____
_____
_____
_____
_____
_____
_____
_____
_____
_____
_____
_____
_____
_____
_____
_____
_____
_____
_____
_____
_____
_____
_____
_____
_____

Date: _____

Holding Space For: _____

Date: _____

Holding Space For: _____

Date: _____

Holding Space For: _____

Date: _____

Holding Space For: _____

Date: _____

Holding Space For: _____

Date: _____

Holding Space For: _____

Date: _____

Holding Space For: _____

"Survival is only the halfway point. The real work begins on the other side."

Date: _____

Holding Space For: _____

_____
_____
_____
_____
_____
_____
_____
_____
_____
_____
_____
_____
_____
_____
_____
_____
_____
_____
_____
_____
_____
_____
_____
_____
_____
_____

"Survival is only the halfway point. The real work begins on the other side."

Date: _____

Holding Space For: _____

Date: _____

Holding Space For: _____

Date: _____

Holding Space For: _____

Date: _____

Holding Space For: _____

Date: _____

Holding Space For: _____

Date: _____

Holding Space For: _____

Date: _____

Holding Space For: _____

Date: _____

Holding Space For: _____

Date: _____

Holding Space For: _____

Date: _____

Holding Space For: _____

Date: _____

Holding Space For: _____

Date: _____

Holding Space For: _____

Date: _____

Holding Space For: _____

Date: _____

Holding Space For: _____

Date: _____

Holding Space For: _____

Date: _____

Holding Space For: _____

Date: _____

Holding Space For: _____

Date: _____

Holding Space For: _____

Date: _____

Holding Space For: _____

"I learned not to kill myself, to keep him alive."

Date: _____

Holding Space For: _____

Date: _____

Holding Space For: _____

Date: _____

Holding Space For: _____

Date: _____

Holding Space For: _____

Date: _____

Holding Space For: _____

Date: _____

Holding Space For: _____

Date: _____

Holding Space For: _____

Date: _____

Holding Space For: _____

Date: _____

Holding Space For: _____

Date: _____

Holding Space For: _____

Date: _____

Holding Space For: _____

Date: _____

Holding Space For: _____

Date: _____

Holding Space For: _____

Date: _____

Holding Space For: _____

Date: _____

Holding Space For: _____

Date: _____

Holding Space For: _____

Date: _____

Holding Space For: _____

Date: _____

Holding Space For: _____

Date: _____

Holding Space For: _____

Date: _____

Holding Space For: _____

"Love is the quiet miracle that keeps us showing up."

Date: _____

Holding Space For: _____

Date: _____

Holding Space For: _____

Date: _____

Holding Space For: _____

Date: _____

Holding Space For: _____

Date: _____

Holding Space For: _____

Date: _____

Holding Space For: _____

Date: _____

Holding Space For: _____

Date: _____

Holding Space For: _____

Date: _____

Holding Space For: _____

Date: _____

Holding Space For: _____

Date: _____

Holding Space For: _____

Date: _____

Holding Space For: _____

Date: _____

Holding Space For: _____

Date: _____

Holding Space For: _____

Date: _____

Holding Space For: _____

Date: _____

Holding Space For: _____

Date: _____

Holding Space For: _____

Date: _____

Holding Space For: _____

Date: _____

Holding Space For: _____

Date: _____

Holding Space For: _____

_____
_____
_____
_____
_____
_____
_____
_____
_____
_____
_____
_____
_____
_____
_____
_____
_____
_____
_____
_____
_____
_____
_____
_____
_____
_____

"Peace doesn't always feel peaceful. Sometimes it's just permission to rest."

Date: _____

Holding Space For: _____

Date: _____

Holding Space For: _____

Date: _____

Holding Space For: _____

Date: _____

Holding Space For: _____

Date: _____

Holding Space For: _____

_____
_____
_____
_____
_____
_____
_____
_____
_____
_____
_____
_____
_____
_____
_____
_____
_____
_____
_____
_____
_____
_____
_____
_____
_____
_____
_____

Date: _____

Holding Space For: _____

Date: _____

Holding Space For: _____

Date: _____

Holding Space For: _____

Date: _____

Holding Space For: _____

Date: _____

Holding Space For: _____

Date: _____

Holding Space For: _____

Date: _____

Holding Space For: _____

Date: _____

Holding Space For: _____

Date: _____

Holding Space For: _____

Date: _____

Holding Space For: _____

Date: _____

Holding Space For: _____

Date: _____

Holding Space For: _____

Date: _____

Holding Space For: _____

Date: _____

Holding Space For: _____

Date: _____

Holding Space For: _____

_____
_____
_____
_____
_____
_____
_____
_____
_____
_____
_____
_____
_____
_____
_____
_____
_____
_____
_____
_____
_____
_____
_____
_____

"Sometimes holding space means saying nothing at all."

Date: _____

Holding Space For: _____

Date: _____

Holding Space For: _____

Date: _____

Holding Space For: _____

Date: _____

Holding Space For: _____

Date: _____

Holding Space For: _____

Date: _____

Holding Space For: _____

Date: _____

Holding Space For: _____

Date: _____

Holding Space For: _____

Date: _____

Holding Space For: _____

Date: _____

Holding Space For: _____

Date: _____

Holding Space For: _____

Date: _____

Holding Space For: _____

Date: _____

Holding Space For: _____

Date: _____

Holding Space For: _____

Date: _____

Holding Space For: _____

_____
_____
_____
_____
_____
_____
_____
_____
_____
_____
_____
_____
_____
_____
_____
_____
_____
_____
_____
_____
_____
_____

"Grief teaches us to listen differently."

Date: _____

Holding Space For: _____

Date: _____

Holding Space For: _____

Date: _____

Holding Space For: _____

Date: _____

Holding Space For: _____

Date: _____

Holding Space For: _____

Date: _____

Holding Space For: _____

Date: _____

Holding Space For: _____

Date: _____

Holding Space For: _____

Thank you for holding space --- for yourself, and for others.

-Deidra

www.ingramcontent.com/pod-product-compliance
Lightning Source LLC
Chambersburg PA
CBHW030449100526
44580CB00002B/43